A nativity pantomime

Michael Forster

First published in 1997 by
KEVIN MAYHEW LTD
Rattlesden
Bury St Edmunds
Suffolk IP30 0SZ

0 1 2 3 4 5 6 7 8 9

ISBN 1 84003 036 4
Catalogue No 1500139

Cover by Darren
Typesetting by Louise Hill
Printed in Great Britain

Foreword

The triumph of good over evil is an essential theme of all pantomimes, so it is not surprising that Christmas has become the traditional time for them to be presented. The format offers an excellent medium for combining entertainment and communication as the audience is stimulated to join in enthusiastically, booing and hissing the evil characters, cheering the good, and generally getting involved in the banter and the action.

Pantomime also appeals because it involves people of all ages: the spontaneous child locked inside the older ones of us can be liberated by the free spirits of the young. So with this show, the whole church and/or community can unite, for in pantomime the audience too are performers. It may well be that many young people in the churches (having outgrown their first childhood and not yet discovered the joy of the second) would not be happy to take part in the traditional Nativity play, but will be delighted to be on stage in a production such as this – or to sit in the audience as rabble-rousers!

In producing this script, I have sought to communicate the essence of the Incarnation: God enters the world in Christ, deliberately choosing to be among the humble, and in making that choice immediately makes himself vulnerable to the evils of the world – personified in Wicked King Herod obsessed with his own wealth and power. The Angel makes clear that good is and will remain supreme over evil, whatever the present setbacks, but plays a subdued role, allowing the hope to grow from within the situation rather than being imposed from without. At the end of the pantomime, Herod is utterly thwarted in his designs and those whom he would oppress and exploit are shown to be in possession of a kind of power which he could never understand.

While having fun at the expense of Herod and the Innkeeper, I have been very careful not to send up the holy family. Joseph (Joe) and Mary are certainly friendly and accessible, but never lose their essential dignity.

MICHAEL FORSTER

Production Notes

Simplicity is the key in all aspects of production. There is no reason why this show should be beyond the resources of an average or smaller church, youth club, etc. However, this should not mean that special talents cannot be used; tailor the show to the resources available and allow people's particular skills to be valued without their feeling over-stretched or threatened.

SETS

One basic set can serve throughout. One of the entrances to the stage should be through a door, the sign over which can be changed as directed in the script to identify the location of different scenes. Part of the stage will then serve as the street or a courtyard outside the inn or the palace, and another area as the stable. I suggest that some sort of low partition be set up in the 'stable' area. The pantomime donkey can then spend most of its time behind this with just the head showing, allowing the person who is the hind legs to sit comfortably out of sight of the audience. If this can't be done, then the donkey should be banished from the stage when not actually required ('Go on, get off with you; we can't have livestock around the baby!'). This will avoid back problems for the 'hind legs'.

COSTUMES

Have fun with these! The exception to that is Mary, and perhaps Joseph, since these characters are not sent up. Mary could wear something like a caftan or other long dress; Joseph should be recognisably a carpenter, perhaps in a modern carpenter's apron with a hammer in his belt. Wicked King Herod should be outlandishly evil looking. The Three Wise Guys are business executives and could wear smart business suits, but with something incongruous about them, such as bizarre headgear with zodiac signs. Widow Swanky should be the archetypal pantomime dame. The real fun will be in designing the costumes according to what strange items of apparel people have hidden away in their attics. The most difficult costume will be that of the donkey. However, some brown or grey cloth to cover the body, along with a couple of pairs of similar coloured trousers, take care of most of it. Designing and making the head could be an activity for a children's or youth group.

DIALOGUE

I have provided the basic structure and dialogue, and this on its own would work well enough. However, in the true spirit of pantomime (and Incarnation, come to that) the show will be best when you take it and make it your own: local references, 'in jokes', allusions perhaps to contemporary events, catch-phrases, etc.

To avoid problems with too much memorising of lines, I suggest using props on which the dialogue can be written. For example, the innkeeper (Widow Swanky) has a clipboard with a 'guest list' on it, Herod a large chocolate box, and the shepherds could carry a lamb. It should be a simple matter to attach a piece of paper to the prop with either Blu-tack or pins as appropriate, and change the paper in between scenes. However, players should use this as a memory-jogger, rather than try to fit all the dialogue on the prop and then read it. Much of the dialogue will be flexible anyway, depending upon the response of the audience, but it might help to write down a few key phrases in each scene.

The introduction at the beginning would best be spoken from off stage, using a microphone, with the room darkened. Appropriate eerie sound effects would enhance it, but are not essential.

MUSIC

Pantomimes are not musicals, and songs play an important but small part in the overall effect. I have offered a few new lyrics set to old tunes for ease of learning. All the tunes for the songs, and the suggested incidental music, can be found in *Top Tunes* (Kevin Mayhew), and these could be played on a keyboard or whatever combination of instruments is available. Alternatively, you may wish to substitute appropriate songs from, for example, the current hit parade in place of some of the ones suggested here. A karaoke machine would be a simple way to do that, but there could be problems with copyright and performing rights which must, of course, be respected.

A number of other songs are suggested at various points, and the Choir of Angels could also be used to lead the singing of a few carols. To avoid difficult mass entries and exits which would spoil the flow of the pantomime, have the Choir of Angels in a fixed place where they can simply stand to sing and sit for the rest of the performance.

Another way of enhancing the show would be to use special tunes to identify different characters, rather in the style of the operatic *leitmotif*. A few bars of the tune could be played when the character enters. Here are some examples, all from *Top Tunes.*

- Widow Swanky   *Humoreske* (Dvořák)
- Mary   *Ave Maria*
- Joe   *The Harmonious Blacksmith*
- Three Wise Guys   *Three Blind Mice*
- Shepherds   *On Ilkley Moor, baht 'at*
- Herod   *Go down, Moses* (or you might like to find some particularly sinister music from another source)
- Angels   *Für Elise*
- Ruth   *Lullaby* (Brahms)

Incidental music also plays an important part, especially in the more dramatic scenes. When the action becomes fast and furious, you might play, for example the *William Tell Overture* or the theme from the Mozart *Horn Concerto*. There are plenty of options, and the only limitations are the available resources and imagination.

SOUND EFFECTS

These can really bring a pantomime to life, but must fit in with the action. A suspended cymbal to strike when anybody falls over is ideal; alternatively, get someone to dangle a saucepan lid by a piece of string while someone else hits it. Again, experiment during rehearsal and let people use their own imaginations.

RABBLE-ROUSING

Audience involvement is vital to a successful production, and it would be worth having one or two well-prepared 'plants' seated anonymously at strategic places who could encourage this by heckling, joining in, etc., at appropriate moments. Again, some suggestions are made in the script, and some of these would certainly need to be led; but do whatever is appropriate in your setting.

BE FLEXIBLE!

As suggested earlier, unnecessary complication is best avoided; work within your own resources. However, this should not stifle initiative where particular talents exist. If, for example, you have a member who is an accomplished juggler, then find an excuse to get them on the stage! If you have more actors than the script allows for, then create a few more characters, but don't let people feel either press-ganged or excluded.

I hope you have lots of fun with this production – it's certainly been enjoyable to write – and that the essential message of Christmas, of God overcoming evil not by mere superior force but by the 'more excellent *way*' of love, will be well communicated in the process.

You could photocopy the poster opposite and get the children to colour it, add your own details of dates, venue, etc., and display in prominent places around the area.

Here are some examples of some props you might construct which the actors could carry, to help them remember their lines.

- Joe   a piece of wood which he carries around 'just in case he fancies doing a bit of carpentry'
- The angel   a harp-shaped piece of plywood or cardboard
- Widow Swanky   a clipboard for the guest list
- Herod   a large chocolate box
- Ruth   various notes she reads out; and she could also conceal prompts in the tops of the treacle buckets
- Shepherds   lambs (either plywood silhouettes or fluffy toys)
- Wise Guys   route map (possibly also on a clipboard), executive-style briefcases

CAST
(in order of appearance)

NARRATOR

JOE

ANGEL

CHOIR OF ANGELS

MARY

ROVER
Joe and Mary's donkey

WIDOW SWANKY
innkeeper

RUTH
Widow Swanky's daughter

WICKED KING HEROD

SHEPHERD 1

SHEPHERD 2

SHEPHERD 3

SALAMI
a slave girl

CASPAR
a wise guy

MELCHIOR
a wise guy

BALTHAZAR
a wise guy

BABY JESUS

SCENE 1

(Courtyard at Nazareth. Sign over door says 'Nazareth Carpentry'. Another part of the stage is a stable area, with a low partition. This is essential so that the rear end of the donkey can be out of view some of the time, allowing the actor to relax.)

Narrator *(Preferably not on view, speaking through PA system)* Come with us to a distant place and a faraway time: to the land ruled over by Wicked King Herod. The people long to be free, but it is a vain hope, for behind the Wicked King Herod is the mightiest and cruellest empire the world has ever seen. Will God not rescue his people from this dreadful tyranny? An ancient prophecy speaks of a new king, to be born in the city of Bethlehem. But *when* will he be born? Who will be his parents? And will he survive in the land of wicked King Herod?

(Enter JOE from inside workshop, wearing a carpenter's apron and carrying a piece of board, sandpapering the edge as he comes.)

Joe 'Lo, kids! My name's Joe. That's my workshop there. Look, d'you want to be my friends? Right. Tell you what we'll do then. Whenever I say, ''Lo, kids!' I want you to say, ''Lo, Joe!' Right? OK, let's practise it.

'Lo, Kids!
('Lo, Joe!)

Is that all of you? Didn't sound very loud to me. Let's try again.

'Lo, Kids!
('Lo, Joe!)

Better. Something's still not right, though, is it? I've got it. There are some people out there who don't think they're kids. Look, this is a panto. Right? So *everybody's* a kid. Don't care how old you are, how many A-levels you've got or which way round you wear your collar. You're here: you're a kid. So let's try again. Ready?

11

'Lo, Kids!
(*'Lo, Joe!*)

(*Enter ANGEL.*)

Angel   'Lo, Joe!

Joe   Oh, no! What do you want?

Angel   That's not a very nice welcome.

Joe   No, I'm sorry. It's just that whenever I think I've got things nicely sorted out, and life's comfortably predictable, *you* always show up and change everything.

Angel   Don't be like that, Joe. I'm just here to give you a message from God. But of course if you don't want to know, don't let me force it on you.

Joe   No, you've started so you'd better finish, I suppose. What is it?

Angel   I just thought you'd like to know – so that you can have time to pack.

Joe   Pack?

Angel   Yes. You're going away.

Joe   Going away? I can't leave Mary just now. She's having a baby, you know.

Angel   'Course I know, Joe. I told *you* that! But don't worry, you aren't going to have to leave her – she's going with you to Bethlehem.

Joe   *Bethlehem?* That's miles away. She can't make that kind of journey.

Angel   Trust me, Joe. You'll get there safely, and so will Mary and the baby. Anyway, you're not going to have any choice you know: it's the Governor's orders.

Joe   But why does God want us –

Angel	Not *the* Guvnor, Joe. The *Roman* Governor. Now you might get away with arguing with God, but the Romans aren't so patient, so I'd get packed if I were you. Don't worry, though. I'll never be far away from you.
Joe	That's a comforting thought!

NO TIME TO ARGUE
(Tune: *Bill Bailey, won't you please come home*)

Choir of Angels	No time, to argue, Joseph, just hit the road! You've got to go today. Leave all your cares behind to lighten the load, trust God to show the way. Now it's beginning, Joseph, this is the hour, you've got no time to hang around: the kingdom of God is coming with pow'r, and Bethlehem is where you're bound.
Joe	But –
Choir of Angels	No time, to argue, Joseph, time to depart, listen to what you hear: don't stop to think about it, just make a start, God will make all things clear. You've got no option, Joseph, you can't decline, because the order comes from Rome, but God can include it in his design, so Joseph, won't you please leave home!

(Enter MARY, excitedly, waving a letter.)

Mary	Joe! Joe! We've had a letter. Look, we've got to go to Bethlehem – isn't it wonderful?
Joe	I know. I thought you'd be horrified.
Mary	No, I'm really glad. That means that our son will be born in Bethlehem.
Joe	I don't see what's so good about Bethlehem.

Mary	But I've often heard you say that it's a great place to come from.
Joe	Exactly. it's a wonderful place to *come from* – and a terrible place to *go to*.
Mary	Oh, don't be such an old misery, Joe. I think it's wonderful, Jesus being born in the same city as King David.
Joe	But we can't go now. I still haven't finished mending the rabbi's cart.
Mary	I thought you'd finished that.
Joe	Only the bodywork – I've still got to do something about the noisy engine.
Donkey *(Off stage)*	Hee haw!
Joe	That's the engine.
Mary	Don't worry, I've talked to the rabbi and he says you can borrow Rover for the journey to Bethlehem.
Joe	Well, that should make things a bit easier, anyway.
Donkey *(Off stage)*	Hee haw!
Joe	Not quieter, mind you, but easier. Look, you go and pack and I'll get Rover ready.
Mary	All right. But be kind to him. He's a thoroughbred, remember.

(Exit MARY.)

Donkey *(Off stage)*	Hee haw!
Joe	*(Calls)* Rover! Come on, Rover!

(Enter ROVER, pantomime donkey.)

Joe   Now, Rover. We're going on a long journey. Won't that be nice?

(ROVER *shakes his head.*)

Joe   And you're going to carry Mary – and the baby, of course.

(ROVER *shakes his head more vigorously.*)

Joe   Oh yes, you are!

(ROVER *shakes his head emphatically four times.*)

Joe   Oh yes, you are!

(ROVER *again shakes his head emphatically four times.*)

Joe   I'm not arguing with you, Rover. You're going, and that's it.

(ROVER *shakes his head emphatically four times and runs off into auditorium. Chase ensues. Suggested Music:* William Tell Overture.)

(*According to space available,* ROVER *might disappear, and* JOE *ask the audience which way he went. Eventually,* ROVER *returns to stage and tries to exit but is blocked by* MARY *entering at same time.*)

Mary   Rover! What on earth's the matter? What are you doing to him, Joe?

Joe   Nothing! I just told him he'd got to go to Bethlehem, and he panicked.

Mary   What's so dreadful about Bethlehem, Rover?

(ROVER *whispers in* MARY's *ear.*)

Mary   Why are you so frightened to be near Jerusalem?

(ROVER *whispers in* MARY's *ear.*)

Mary	Wicked King Herod? Oh, he won't bother us. We're much too unimportant for that.

(MARY and ROVER converse in whispers as JOE addresses audience.)

Joe	Tell you what, Rover. We'll get my gang on side, shall we? 'Lo, kids!

('Lo, Joe!)

	You'll keep watch for us, won't you? And tell us if Wicked King Herod comes near us?
Mary	They don't know what he looks like.
Joe	Oh, they'll know him. You can't miss Wicked King Herod. OK, kids?
Mary	Well, it doesn't matter anyway, because Rover says he'll come.
Joe	What changed his mind?
Mary	I threatened to change his name – to Morris.
Joe	We'd better get started, I suppose. I just hope that we can get a room at the inn.

(Exeunt MARY, JOE and ROVER into auditorium. As they process round, the Choir of Angels could lead the singing of a song such as 'Little Donkey'.)

SCENE 2

(Courtyard of the Ass and Emperor, Bethlehem. Change by simply reversing sign outside workshop to read 'The Ass and Emperor' and erecting another sign by 'Stable' area.)

(Enter WIDOW SWANKY, pantomime dame, checking off a list of guests on a clipboard.)

Swanky   Now, let me see. I've got the Smiths in the attic, and the Joneses down below. That'll please the Smiths. And I've got that nice Mr Jacob in the annexe, and Mr Amos next door. I've just got to find room for Mr Isaacs. Let's see . . . Oh, of course – I can put him to share with Mr Amos. Well, Mr Amos works nights, so neither of them will ever know. Business is business, after all. That's it, then – full up – no more room.

(Enter RUTH, carrying two buckets.)

Ruth   *(Loudly)* What shall I do with these buckets of –

Swanky   Water! Put them on the landing where the fire buckets belong.

Ruth   *(Loudly)* No, they're not water, they're –

Swanky   Well, sand then. Take them inside, Ruth, and put them somewhere safe.

(RUTH begins to go towards inn entrance. SWANKY mops her brow in relief. Behind her, RUTH stops, looking puzzled, and scratches her head.)

Swanky   My word, that was close. That's my daughter Ruth. She's not very bright, but she's a lovely girl. You won't believe this, but I was a really hard woman before I had her. Ruthless, I was. Absolutely Ruthless. Now where was I? *(Examines clipboard)*

Ruth   *(Loudly)* But the buckets have got treacle in them!

Swanky	*(Jumping with astonishment)* What are you doing still there? Now you've gone and given the game away, and I'm going to have to tell all these people the truth. You go in there and hide those buckets. You never know who's around.

(Exit RUTH. SWANKY turns to audience.)

Swanky	Oh well, you look like an honest lot to me, most of you anyway. *(Leans forward and beckons conspiratorially)* You see, Wicked King Herod hates children. But he loves sweets, so he's banned children from having any sweets so there'll be more for him. But what he doesn't know is that I make sweets in a secret factory in my inn. And then I go round the town leaving sweets on the children's doorsteps. But if Herod ever found out he'd kill me. And the children. Tell you what: would you like to help?
	Good. Then you can be my security guards. If ever you see Wicked King Herod coming, you let me know. All right? Let's practise that. I want you to pretend you've seen Wicked King Herod, and boo and hiss as loudly as you can. Got it? Go!
	Well, that wasn't bad, but I think you can do better than that, can't you? Try again.
	That was *much* better. And remember, whatever happens he mustn't get into the inn. So if he goes anywhere near there you really must tell me. OK? Good. Now, if you'll excuse me I've got to get on because –

(Enter HEROD: children boo and hiss.)

Swanky	Yes, that's right, dears. That was wonderful, but you don't need to practise any more. Save yourselves for when it really matters.
Audience	He's behind you!
Swanky	What's that?
Audience	He's behind you!

Swanky   Eh? I'm sorry, I can't hear when you're all shouting at once. Now hush, d'you hear?

(Order is eventually restored.)

Swanky   Right, that's better. Now, you: *(Points to child)* what were you saying?

          (Child: He's behind you.)

(Exit HEROD.)

Swanky   *(Checking)* No, he's not. You're playing jokes on me.

(Enter HEROD. Stands close up behind SWANKY. As children shout again, SWANKY turns about, first left, then right. HEROD moves with her and she doesn't see him.)

Swanky   You're teasing me. And I thought you were my friends. You're horrible, you are.

(SWANKY goes to side of stage opposite stable and sulks. HEROD then moves towards inn.)

Children   He's going to the inn!

(SWANKY turns and sees HEROD.)

Swanky   Well, bless my great big woolly socks, it's King Hardup.

Herod   Herod!

Swanky   *(Shaking HEROD's hand vigorously)* Swanky – Mrs – pleased to make your acquaintance.

Herod   *(Impatiently removing his hand)* Don't play games with me, Widow Planky. You know why I'm here.

Swanky   I do! I mean, I *do?*

Herod	I know that you're making sweets here, and not giving me any. I know that you're giving them to horrible, selfish, spoilt, cheeky, disrespectful children.
Swanky	*(To audience)* He knows my family.
Herod	Never mind the wisecracks, Widow Cranky.
Swanky	You mean Swanky.
Herod	I know what I mean. Just you remember that if ever I catch you making sweets, I'll confiscate your confectionery. Got it?
Swanky	Oh, I don't mind that – just as long as you don't take my sweets.
Herod	Sweets?
Swanky	Just a joke, King Fed-up.
Herod	Herod!
Swanky	Swanky – Mrs – pleased to make your acquaintance. *(Shakes HEROD's hand vigorously)*
Herod	*(Impatiently removing his hand)* Don't *do* that! I'm going back to the palace.
Swanky	Ooh, that's nice. I used to go there when I was a little dame.
Herod	You've never been to the palace.
Swanky	Yes, I have. All us girls used to put our handbags in the middle and dance round them. Lovely, it was.
Herod	That was the Palais, not the Palace.
Swanky	*(Sings)* You say the Palais, and I say the Palace,
	You go to Calais, and I go to Callas.
Herod	Palais –
Swanky	Palace –
Herod	Calais –

Swanky	Callas –
Herod	Let's call the whole thing off –
	What am I doing! Look here, Widow Blankie –
Swanky	Swanky.
Herod	*(Shaking her hand vigorously)* Herod – King – pleased to meet you. This is ridiculous!
Swanky	And I'd like to say what a pleasure it is to meet you.
Herod	Thank you.
Swanky	But I can't, 'cos it's not.
Herod	You just enjoy your bit of fun, Swanky Doodle, but one day you'll laugh on the other side of your face. I'll find those sweets, or my name's not King Hairdo.
Swanky	Herod.
Herod	Mark my words, Widow Swanky. I shall return.

(Exit HEROD.)

(Enter JOE, still carrying his wooden board, and MARY.)

Mary	Really, Joe! I don't know why you had to bring that piece of wood with you.
Joe	Well, you never know, I might want to do a bit of carpentry while we're here. After all, what else am I going to do while you're having the baby? *(Mary shrugs her shoulders in despair)* Hey, look – there's my gang! 'Lo, kids!
	('Lo, Joe!)
Swanky	Can I help you?
Mary	I'm Mary, and this is my husband Joseph. I think we've got a room booked?
Swanky	*(Consulting clipboard)* No, I'm sorry. No Mary and Joseph down here.

Mary	Oh, don't say the post didn't arrive again!
Joe	When I catch that pigeon, I'll privatise it!
Mary	So, you haven't got a room, then?
Swanky	Room? I haven't even got a cupboard. It's the same everywhere.

NO ROOM
(Tune: *Camptown Races*)

Swanky	In Bethlehem, we sing this song: 'No room! No room!' The waiting lists are five miles long, 'No room at the inn!' Got to search all night, got to search all day.
Mary and Joseph	We know that God won't let us down, we've got a child on the way.
Swanky	The people search, but all in vain, 'No room! No room!' We always sing this sad refrain: 'No room at the inn!' Got to search all night, got to search all day.
Mary and Joseph	We know that God won't let us down, we've got a child on the way.

Joe	But there must be *somewhere* you can put us. I know. *(To audience)* Can *you* think of anything?
Children	What about the stable?
Joe	What was that?
Children	What about the stable?

Joe	Oh, no! I don't think God would want us to let Jesus be born in a stable.
Swanky	He might.
Joe	Oh no, he wouldn't!
Children	Oh yes, he would!
Joe	Oh no, he wouldn't!
Children	Oh yes, he would!
Mary	Come on, Joe. If it's all there is, it'll just have to do.
Joe	Oh, very well. Where's the ass?
Swanky	Oh, don't you worry about King Herod. He left before you came.
Joe	Not that ass – the donkey – Rover. Where is he?
Mary	He's outside. *(Calls)* Rover! Here!

(Enter ROVER.)

Joe	Now, Rover, we're sharing your stable tonight, so you're going to go over there, behind that partition.

(ROVER shakes head emphatically four times.)

Joe	Oh yes, you are!

(ROVER shakes head emphatically four times.)

Joe	Oh yes, you are!

(ROVER shakes head emphatically four times.)

Mary	Oh yes, you are – *Morris*.

(ROVER nods head emphatically four times and trots round behind partition and stands looking over it. Rear end of donkey can now relax, out of view of audience.)

Swanky	He must be really tired – you've come a long way.
Joe	Yes . . .

IT'S A LONG WAY TO CARRY MARY
(Tune: *It's a long way to Tipperary*)

Joe	It's a long way to carry Mary, it's a long way to go. It's a long way to carry Mary, on the roughest road I know. Nowhere to get a sandwich, or a cup of tea: It's a long, long way to carry Mary, for Rover and me.

Mary	*(Smiling)* All right, smart Alec! let's get this place ship-shape.

(Enter RUTH.)

Ruth	Here! Herod's coming back.
Swanky	Herod? *(Turns to MARY)* And you with a baby on the way. You've got to hide.

(General panic ensues.)

Joe	The stable!
Swanky	No, he'll see you!
Mary	The inn!
Swanky	He's probably coming to search it.
Joe	I know: my gang! Will you hide us, kids?

(JOE and MARY hide in audience.)

(Enter HEROD.)

Swanky	Well, well, well, King Hairpsray.
Herod	Herod!
Swanky	*(Shaking his hand vigorously)* Swanky – Widow – pleased to meet you.
Herod	Don't start all that again. I've come back because . . . *(Sniffs conspicuously)* What can I smell?
Swanky	What? Nothing. Oh, probably the donkey.
Herod	No – something sweet.
Swanky	Probably his tooth.
Herod	Don't you play games with me.
Ruth	*(Stage whisper)* I've put the buckets of –
Swanky	I know, the fire buckets are on the landing.
Ruth	No, I meant –
Swanky	Why don't you run along and check they're not leaking? NOW!

(Exit RUTH.)

Herod	*(Walking over to stand near ROVER)* What's this? Something you've rescued from the abattoir?

(ROVER starts getting agitated.)

Swanky	I'm, er, looking after him for a friend.
Herod	Well, if your friend doesn't come back, I'll buy him from you. I'd get a good price selling him on to the glue factory.

(Enter RUTH with a piece of paper.)

Ruth	Message for King Herod. You're needed at the palace.
Herod	Oh, what is it this time?

Ruth	Important visitors. From Yorkshire.
Herod	Yorkshire?
Ruth	That's what it says here. *(Reads)* 'Three wise guys from the East Riding.'
Swanky	Give me that! *(Reads)* 'Three wise guys from the East, riding on camels.'
Herod	Tell them I'm coming. *(Exit RUTH)* But I'll be back, Widow Swanky. I'm going to trace the source of that sweet smell, and when I do you'll find out how treacle feels when it's melting slowly in a cauldron.

(Exit HEROD.)

(Enter JOE and MARY.)

Mary	I don't like the sound of him.
Swanky	Oh, don't worry. I can handle old Henpecked. He's been after me for years and never caught me yet. I just hope you'll be warm enough in the stable; it looks like being a cold night.

(MARY and JOSEPH move to stable area and inspect it. Then all characters slip offstage for the scene change.)

SCENE 3

(Moors at night. Change sign to 'Sheep Fold'. The lights should be turned down.)

(Enter two SHEPHERDS.)

Shepherd 1	Those sheep are quiet tonight.
Shepherd 2	Yes. Strange for the time of year.
Shepherd 1	*(Peers towards audience)* Are there any there?
Shepherd 2	*(Peers towards audience)* Yes, look – rows and rows of 'em.
Shepherd 1	They don't *sound* like sheep.
Shepherd 2	Oh I'm sure they could if they tried. Come on, then. Give me a 'baah'!
	(Baah!)
Shepherd 1	Did you hear anything?
Shepherd 2	Don't think so.
Shepherd 1	Try again.
Shepherd 2	Give me a 'baah'!
	(Baah!)
Shepherd 1	Ah, that's better. Well, I suppose we're in for another long, cold, boring night. I get really fed up with this job.
Shepherd 2	I'll cheer you up. What do sheep think of Christmas?
Shepherd 1	I don't know. What *do* sheep think of Christmas?
Shepherd 2	Bah! Humbug!
Shepherd 1	*(Groans)*
Shepherd 2	All right, then: why did the shepherd get arrested?

Shepherd 1	I know, I know: for hiding a crook. I can't cope with this. Please, won't somebody save me!

(Enter ANGEL: full lighting.)

Angel	You called?

(SHEPHERDS crouch down and cover their eyes.)

Shepherd 2	You and your big mouth! Now look what you've done.
Shepherd 1	It wasn't me telling awful jokes.
Angel	Don't be afraid. I've got good news for you. You were asking to be saved, weren't you? Well, your Saviour has arrived.

(SHEPHERDS rise to their feet.)

Shepherd 1	What? A gag writer for him? Or just a 'gag' would do.
Angel	Oh, better than that. A new King: one who's going to be on the side of the little people – stand up for the ones who get pushed around.
Shepherd 2	Herod's not going to like that.
Angel	You leave Herod to us. Now d'you want to be part of this, or not? Because if you do you'd better get off to Bethlehem. You'll find the new King lying in a manger in the stable at Widow Swanky's place.
Shepherd 1	Now come on: when did anything good come out of Widow Swanky's stable?
Angel	God can bring something good out of *anywhere*.

GLORIA
(Tune: *The Entertainer*)

Choir of Angels	Praise and glory to God on high, goodwill and peace to his people on earth!

Praise and glory to God on high,
let the universe glorify his name!
Praise and glory to God on high,
goodwill and peace to his people on earth!
Praise and glory to God,
eternal glory to God,
eternal glory to God the most high!

Shepherd 1   Well, come on, then. Let's go.

Shepherd 2   What about the sheep? What if the wolves get them?

Shepherd 1   *(Peering at audience)* What? That lot? If you ask me, it's the wolves we should be protecting, not them!

(Exeunt SHEPHERDS.)

SCENE 4

(HEROD's Palace. Change sign to read 'The Palais: Royal Sweet'.)

(Enter HEROD, who returns the boos and hisses from the audience, then claps his hands.)

(Enter SALAMI, a slave girl.)

Herod   Ah, Salami! There you are at last. Where are these Three Wise Guys, then?

Salami   They're waiting outside.

Herod   Well, show them in, Salami. And how often must I tell you to get that sign changed? *(Points to sign over door)*

Salami   Yes, Your Majesty. I'll call the court magician.

Herod   No, not him. Can't spell for toffee. And talking of toffee, where are my sweets? This box is nearly empty.

Salami   There seems to be a supply problem, Your Majesty. I gather that the children have somehow managed to get hold of them.

Herod   Children? *Children?* You mean that perfectly good toffees, and lovely creamy chocolates, and delicious sticky lollipops are being wasted on *children*? I'll put a stop to that, just as soon as I've got rid of these Three Wise Guys.

(Exit SALAMI.)

Herod   So. The children are getting sweets, are they? That Widow Swanky's at the bottom of this, and I'm going to get her one day. *(Peers out into auditorium)* And if I ever see any children eating sweets . . .

(Enter SALAMI with THREE WISE GUYS who are arguing over the map.)

Caspar   Say, is this a map or a long-lost Picasso?

Melchior   I told you we should have turned left back there.

30

Balthazar	That's the A47, and it's a nightmare. We're better off keeping on the old road.
Salami	Your Majesty: may I present the Three Wise Guys?
Caspar	Pleased to meet you, Kingy, baby. Say, are those all your own teeth, or are you breaking them in for a camel?
Balthazar	Allow us to introduce ourselves.

THREE WISE GUYS
(Tune: *Three Blind Mice*)

Wise guys	Three wise guys, three wise guys, led by a star, led by a star. And if you're wondering who we are,
Melchior	we're Melchior,
Caspar	Caspar,
Balthazar	and Balthazar.
Melchior	We're healthy,
Caspar	we're wealthy,
Balthazar	we're
Herod	truly bizarre!
Wise guys	We're three wise guys. Three wise guys, three wise guys, led by a star, led by a star. You'll find us very good company, with plenty of banter and repartee.
Melchior	We're witty,
Caspar	we're pretty,

Balthazar	we're staying to tea,
All three	we're three wise guys.
	Three wise guys, three wise guys, led by a star, led by a star. We've crossed the desert to see the King, we've got him some presents and everything,
Melchior	we're racy,
Caspar	we're pacey,
Balthazar	we're having a fling,
All three	we're three wise guys.

Herod	So, tell me your business.
Melchior	We're tycoons in the computer industry, and you know what that makes us?
Herod	No.
Balthazar	Electronic magnates.
Caspar	It's the way he tells 'em!
Herod	Have you always been in computers?
Balthazar	No. We used to have a shepherding business, but it failed.
Herod	Why?
Melchior	Couldn't get the staffs.
Caspar	Boom, boom!
Herod	What's this about a star?
Melchior	Des O'Connor – he's on at the Grand.
Balthazar	But we're really looking for the King.
Herod	*I'm* the king.

Melchior	No, a new-born one.
Caspar	*You* were born yesterday.
Herod	*(Aside to audience)* So! A child who's after my sweets *and* my throne. I know. I'll use these wise guys to help me track him down so that I can get rid of him. *(Turns to WISE GUYS, smiling sweetly)* Perhaps I can help you. *(Claps hands)*

(Enter SALAMI.)

Herod	Tell me, Salami, do you have any knowledge of a new king being born in these parts?
Salami	I don't think so – unless he's the one that's been prophesied.
Herod	Prophesied?
Salami	Yes. According to the prophet, there is going to be a new king born in Bethlehem – one who will save the people from –
Herod	Thank you, Salami, that is all.
Salami	It's in the book of –
Herod	I said, that is all, Salami.
Salami	Yes, Your Majesty.

(Exit SALAMI.)

Herod	Salami's nice, but a little goes a long way. So, gentlemen, it appears that you ought to be looking in Bethlehem. And when you find this *lovely* child, do come back and tell me where he is, won't you? I've got something very special I'd like to do to – for him.

(Exeunt WISE GUYS.)

Herod	Something *really* special. *(Laughs evilly)*

(Exit HEROD.)

SCENE 5

(The Inn: 'The Ass and Emperor' sign is displayed. ROVER is still looking over partition; JOE and MARY sit in stable area beside the manger. MARY is holding the baby; JOE is still sanding his board.)

Mary   Isn't he lovely? You know, Joe, this makes all the hassle of getting here worth while. This little fellow's going to change the world.

Joe   He's made a good start so far – he's turned *our* world upside down.

Mary   Everything seems so much brighter and more hopeful, now. I suppose we shouldn't be surprised, though. All that's happened is that God's kept his promise. Oh, look at his tiny little fingers!

Joe   He's got carpenter's hands.

Mary   Oh, trust you! What he does when he grows up will be up to him – and God. Anyway, that's a long way off; let's just enjoy him.

Joe   Couldn't agree more. And when we get home I'm going to make him a proper cradle – not like this manger.

Mary   That'll be good, Joe, but don't knock this; I actually think there's something rather special about it.

IT'S THE SIMPLEST OF MANGERS
(Tune: *The Last Rose of Summer*)

Mary   It's the simplest of cradles,
but it's fit for a lord;
there's more love in this hovel
than a palace affords!
As his home is a stable,
and his crib is a stall,
he's at home with the homeless,
and at one with us all.

In a world of false riches
that will crumble to dust,
he is born with a fortune
in compassion and trust.
He's a king in a palace
with no bound'ries or walls,
for his home's where his heart is,
and his heart's with us all.

All the hopes of the ages
in this manger are laid,
and the glories of heaven
in this stable displayed;
and this child will be faithful
to his destiny's call,
till his home is established
in the hearts of us all.

(Enter SWANKY.)

Swanky   Well, what an exciting night! Not every night we get babies born in the stable! I could do with forty winks. *(Starts winking)* One, two, three – oh dear, I think that's enough exercise for one night. I'll do the other eye tomorrow. Now let's see: who was it wanted the early call? *(Checks clipboard)*

(Loud knocking at door.)

Swanky   Who can that be at this time of night? *(Calls)* Ruth!

(Enter RUTH.)

Ruth   Yes?

Swanky   Go and answer the door.

Ruth   What?

Swanky   Answer the door!

Ruth	But it isn't saying anything.

(Loud knocking at door.)

Swanky	It is now. Go on!

(Exit RUTH.)

Swanky	I don't know what I'm going to do with that girl. I hope it's not Herod at the door; I've got forty litres of ice cream in the oven, and it just won't set.

(Enter RUTH.)

Ruth	There's a couple of strange people at the door.
Swanky	I haven't got time for the clergy now – I'm busy.
Ruth	They say they've had a message that there's a baby here who's in danger.
Swanky	Danger? What danger? I keep a clean stable, I do. *Rooms* aren't up to much, but the stable's always spotless. Oh, I'd better talk to them. Bring them in.

(Exit RUTH, re-entering immediately with the SHEPHERDS.)

Swanky	What's this about the baby being in danger?

(SHEPHERDS exchange blank looks.)

Ruth	That's what you said to me.
Shepherd 1	I said it was in a *manger*.
Ruth	Well how was I to know?
Shepherd 2	We've been sent by an angel.
Swanky	A likely story! Angels don't talk to scruffy characters like you. If this baby's important enough for angels to take an interest, they'd have told priests, not shepherds.

Shepherd 3	Perhaps we were the only ones who were awake.
Swanky	Cheeky! Look, I don't know who you are, or what you've been taking, but you haven't seen any angel.
Shepherds	Oh yes, we have!
Swanky	Oh no, you haven't!

(SHEPHERDS encourage children to join in . . .)

(JOE comes from stable into courtyard.)

Joe	'Lo Kids!
	('Lo, Joe!)
	Now, what's all this noise about?
Shepherd 1	We've come to see a baby in a manger.
Shepherd 2	An angel told us.
Joe	He must have meant Jesus. Come on in and see him.

(SHEPHERDS follow JOE into stable area and admire baby.)

Swanky	Hey! You be careful – babies need to be kept clean, you know. Huh! Angel indeed! Whatever next?

(Loud knocking at door.)

Swanky	Ruth!
Ruth	I know, I know.

(Exit RUTH, immediately re-entering with THREE WISE GUYS.)

Caspar	Well, hello! Are you married, or is this my unlucky day?
Swanky	I bet you say that to all the girls.
Caspar	I would, but I haven't met all the girls. Now, where's the baby, baby?

Swanky	In the manger, manger. What have you got there?
Melchior	We've brought him presents. I've got gold, because he's a king and a king must have gold.
Caspar	I've got frankincense.
Swanky	What's frankincense?
Caspar	It's like ordinary incense, but less tactful.
Balthazar	And I've got myrrh.
Swanky	Myrrh?
Balthazar	Myrrh than everybody else.
Swanky	How did you know about the baby? Don't say an angel told *you*, too?
Balthazar	Angel? What d'you think we are, nuts or something?
Swanky	Thank goodness!
Melchior	No, you see there was this big star in the sky –
Swanky	Oh, good grief! Spare me the details and go on in.

(WISE GUYS go into stable area; mime offering of gifts, conversation with shepherds and family.)

SONG
Child in the manger or *Away in a manger*

(RUTH begins to leave.)

Swanky	Where d'you think you're going?
Ruth	To bed.
Swanky	Bed? Bed? And let all those poor children down? You've got to help me make the sweets.

Ruth	At this time of night?
Swanky	You know very well this is the only time we can be sure that Herod isn't going to raid us. Now get your pinny on.
Ruth	*(Pointing to audience)* What about them?
Swanky	Them? You can't ask them – they've paid for their tickets, they have. And they're probably going to ask for their money back as it is.
Ruth	They might *like* to help make sweets.
Swanky	Oh no, they wouldn't.
Ruth	Oh yes, they would.
Swanky	Oh no, they wouldn't.
Audience	Oh yes, we would!
Swanky	Oh no, you wouldn't!

(Invite children up on stage and set up portable tables, etc. Give the children overalls to wear and let them get in a thoroughly happy mess 'making sweets'.* The stable party can also join in the fun, Mary watching from the side and holding the baby.)

(Enter ANGEL.)

Angel	Hello, everybody.
Shepherd 1	That's the one! That's the angel we saw.
Swanky	Oh, is it now! And just what sort of an angel are you, consorting with the likes of them?
Angel	The sort that looks out for old sinners like you, Widow Swanky.
Swanky	Who're you calling old?
Caspar	I like your style, baby! Say, are those wings real or did you win them in a raffle?

* Obviously safety is paramount here; make something simple and not involving heat, such as peppermint creams.

Angel	I've come with a warning about Wicked King Herod.
Shepherd 2	Herod! I'm out of here! Come on!

(Exeunt SHEPHERDS.)

Swanky	What were you saying about King Herod?
Angel	He's on the warpath.
Caspar	On the warpath? And – don't tell me – he's got no reservations.
Angel	I'd cut the wisecracks and get going if I were you. And get these children somewhere safe, as well.

(CHILDREN return to auditorium and WISE GUYS take their leave.)

Mary	What about us? What do you want us to do?
Angel	You're to go to Egypt.
Joe	*Egypt!*
Mary	Let's not argue, Joe. *(To Angel)* We'll do whatever you say. God's not let us down yet.
Angel	Well said. Now everything's going to be OK; I'll let you know when it's safe for you to go home.
Mary	*(Calls)* Rover! Over here!

(ROVER comes to main stage area.)

Mary	You're going with us to Egypt.

(ROVER shakes head emphatically four times.)

Mary	Oh yes, you are.

(ROVER shakes head emphatically four times.)

Mary	*(To audience)* Help me, children!

(Children join with MARY: 'Oh yes, you are!')

Angel   Of course, you could always leave him here. Didn't Herod want to sell him to the glue factory?

(ROVER nods head emphatically four times. MARY, JOE and ROVER begin their journey to Egypt, walking round the auditorium and greeting the children on the way, while SWANKY and RUTH wave them off. After a suitable interval, JOE and MARY leave, carrying Jesus.)

Angel   And now you, Widow Swanky.

Swanky   Oh, I'll be all right. I can handle Wicked King Hairbrain.

Angel   I know, but I think you should get this place tidied up before he comes, don't you?

Swanky   The sweets! If he sees them he'll kill me!

(Exit ANGEL. RUTH and SWANKY dash about in a chaotic manner and just manage to get all the debris out of the way in time. SWANKY leans on a wall and gasps for air. RUTH goes into inn.)

Herod   *(Offstage)* Fee, fie, foe, fum! I smell the sweetness of sugarplum!

Swanky   Thank goodness we managed to hide it all in time.

(Enter RUTH, carrying two buckets.)

Ruth   What shall I do with this sticky treacle?

Swanky   What! Get rid of it! Here, give me one of them!

(SWANKY and RUTH dash frantically round the stage with the buckets, as if vainly seeking a hiding place.)

Ruth   What are we going to do?

Swanky   I don't know! Look, it's all gooey and runny!

Ruth   We've got to get rid of the treacle.

Swanky   Throw it away!

Ruth   Shall we?

Swanky   After three, then.

(They turn toward the audience and aim their buckets.)

Swanky   One . . . two . . . three!

(Together, they throw the contents of the buckets, which turn out to be individually wrapped sweets, into the audience.)

(Enter HEROD.)

Herod   I know your secret, Widow Swanky. You're making sweets on these premises.

Swanky   Oh no, I'm not.

Herod   Oh yes, you are!

(HEROD catches sight of audience.)

Herod   Aaagggh! Children! Horrible, sweet-loving children! I'll turn all of you into –

(Enter ANGEL.)

Angel   Oh no, you won't!

Herod   *(Still with back to Angel)* Oh yes, I will!

Angel   Come on, children!

                    (Oh no, you won't!)

(HEROD turns round and starts in fear when he sees the Angel.)

Angel   Your days are numbered, Herod. The baby King you were afraid of is no longer here. He'll grow up to be a better man than you could be in a million years. And when he claims his throne, it will be good news for the Widow Swankys of this world. The earth belongs to the ordinary people you despise, Herod. And from now on, no one need go in fear of you and of people like you. Jesus is going to set the world free from all the evil, corruption and fear that you represent. There's a new world beginning, and all because of a simple young couple and their baby who was born in this very stable.

Swanky   That's it! I'll put up a sign: 'Jesus was born here'. Why, I'll make a fortune out of this. Then I'll be able to be powerful and get away with being horrible, just like Wicked King Hairpiece.

Angel   Tell her, children.

Children   Oh no, you won't!

Swanky   No, you're right. I won't! Toffee, anybody?

IN A MANGER, IN A STABLE
(Tune: *Clementine*)

Angel   In a manger, in a stable,
in a humble little town,
God the King, as God the baby,
turned our values upside down.

Choir of Angels   Hallelujah, hallelujah,
God of high, eternal worth;
let your glory fill the heavens,
and your peace surround the earth.

(Enter MARY and JOE, with the baby.)

Mary   Blessèd is our God and Saviour,
by his humble people praised;
at whose voice the mighty tremble,
by whose hand the poor are raised.

Choir of Angels   Hallelujah, hallelujah,
God of high, eternal worth;
let your glory fill the heavens,
and your peace surround the earth.

Mary	By his strength the proud are scattered, and the worldly wise confused; he has satisfied the hungry, but the rich have been refused.
Choir of Angels	Hallelujah, hallelujah, God of high, eternal worth; let your glory fill the heavens, and your peace surround the earth.
Mary	God has saved his chosen people, all our anxious hearts are stilled: he is constant in his mercy, and his promise is fulfilled
Choir of Angels	Hallelujah, hallelujah, God of high, eternal worth; let your glory fill the heavens, and your peace surround the earth.

THE END

Also by Michael Forster

SINGING, DANCING CARPENTER

Text and lyrics: Michael Forster
Music: Christopher Tambling

This is a musical which celebrates Jesus' life in all its fullness. A full-stage version lasting two hours requires soloists, a chorus and a pianist (and we have band parts for bigger productions). A mini-musical or cantata version lasts 30-40 minutes and provides flexible parts for soloists, groups of singers and the whole choir.

EXODUS

Text and lyrics: Michael Forster
Music: Christopher Tambling

This musical is about the Exodus tradition – that God leads us on a journey of liberation which does not always proceed as we would choose. It has parts for eleven principals (including two non-singing parts) and choruses of Israelites, Egyptians and young revellers.

WOT! NO WINE?

Text and lyrics: Michael Forster
Music: Andrew Moore

Everyone knows the story of how Jesus turned water into wine at a party, but few realise that the wine shortage was no accident . . . This is the story of the Wedding at Cana told as only Michael Forster can tell it. The vocal part is mostly unison with some solos and a few optional SATB sections. The running time is about 40 minutes.

ACT ONE and *ACT TWO*

Each book contains 45 short dramas based on well-known stories from both the Old and New Testaments. Ideal for use in all-age worship, the stories have been imaginatively rewritten with humour and valuable insights while retaining and emphasising the original meaning. The dialogue is deliberately modern to make the characters as recognisably like real people as possible.